1 and 2 Chronicles Enrichment Magazine

IN THIS ISSUE . . .

To the Director

This student folder contains nine study leaflets and the enrichment magazine. Remove the center staple and distribute the leaflets as indicated in the leaders guide. This magazine should be distributed at the first session for use throughout the course.

3558 S. Jefferson Ave., St. Louis, MO 63118-3968

1-800-325-3040 • www.cph.org

Written by Reed Lessing; "The Assyrian Empire" written by Brian Chisamore

Edited by Brian Chisamore

COVER: *King Solomon*, by Maestro de Becerril, ca. 1525. Fine Art Images/Fine Art Images

Graphic design by Christina Ensign

This publication may be available in braille, in large print, or on cassette tape for the visually impaired. Please allow 8 to 12 weeks for delivery. Write to Lutheran Braille Workers, P.O. Box 5000, Yucaipa, CA 92399; call toll-free 1-800-925-6092; or visit the website: www.LBWinc.org.

Manufactured in the United States of America

1 2 3 4 5 6 7 8 9 10 23 22 21 20 19 18 17 16 15 14

Knowing the End Changes Everything

© iStockphoto.com

Sometimes, tasks can be hard to accomplish. Some things in life can be very difficult for us to get through. Even though we know an activity may be good for us, we will put it off as long as possible before we finally wade our way through it. You might feel that way as you read through 1 and 2 Chronicles. Such a feeling would not be hard to understand. These two books are some of the longest in the Bible, and there is an extended genealogy in the first nine chapters of 1 Chronicles. This is followed by narratives full of statistics, temple and religious reform, and names and places that are not part of our everyday vocabulary. These can be difficult books to study.

Quickly Overwhelmed

Most of us haven't heard too many sermons from 1 and 2 Chronicles, and this is probably your first Bible study on these books. It is also safe to assume that growing up, you did not attend very many Sunday School classes or Vacation Bible School events where 1 and 2 Chronicles were the main focus of attention. After two or three weeks of this study, you might feel as though you've had enough, saying "Thank you very much, but I quit!"

And isn't this how life goes sometimes? We find ourselves in a challenging job or a difficult relationship, and we feel overwhelmed. Soon, we set up camp by the trail and sit down to moan and groan about how worthless the whole thing seems to be. On the outside, we may keep up our normal routine; but on the inside, all we want to do is give up. Then we settle for sameness, safety, and the status quo. Comfort, complacency, and convenience become our watchwords. Before we know it, we are stuck in a tight radius of don'ts, won'ts, can'ts, and quits.

When we feel discouraged, we need someone to direct us away from our present pain and help us see our

© Joe Belanger/iStockphoto.com

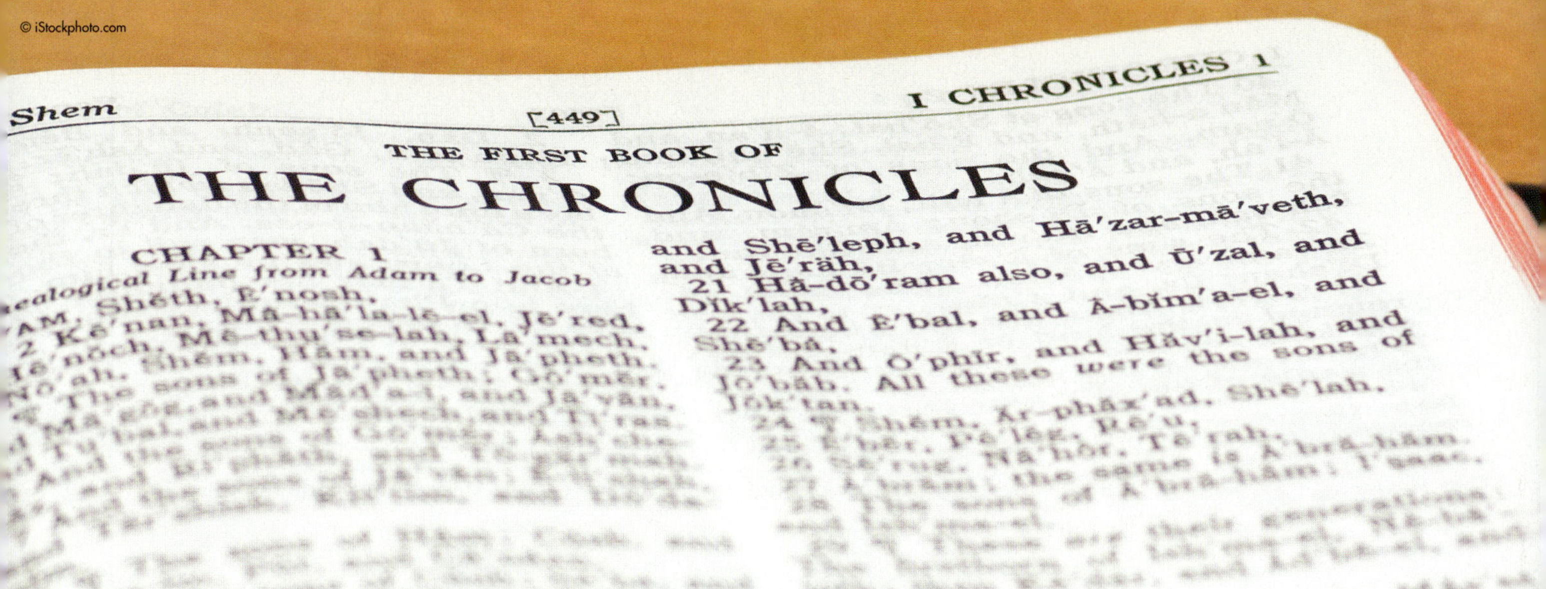

future deliverance. Thankfully, we have this kind of assistance in studying these books of Scripture! Fast forwarding to the end of 1 and 2 Chronicles, we encounter these words:

> *Thus says Cyrus king of Persia, "The Lord, the God of heaven, has given me all the kingdoms of the earth, and He has charged me to build Him a house at Jerusalem, which is in Judah. Whoever is among you of all His people, may the Lord his God be with him. Let him go up."* (2 Chronicles 36:23)

After the devastation and destruction, the death and mourning, the crying and pain written on every page in 1 and 2 Chronicles, there will be a new temple, built in Jerusalem, for God's people. A new day will dawn!

A Good End for Us

Not only does the Book of 2 Chronicles have a blessed end, but we know that we will as well. God's final Word for us is also a rebuilt temple. Jesus Christ, God's temple in human flesh (John 2:19–21), was crushed on Good Friday but raised on Easter morning. In Christ, we walk in newness of life—where darkness is scattered, gloom is gone, and the night of terror and dread is banished.

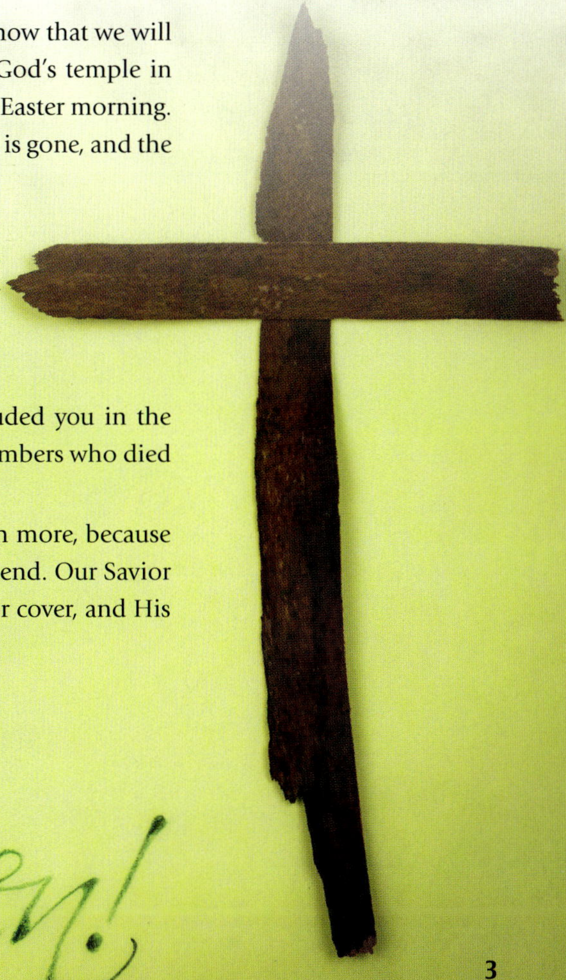

But there is more. When Christ returns, He will be our new temple in the New Jerusalem (as we read in Revelation 21:22), restoring everything we have lost. All our years of pain will be erased, every tear of disappointment will be wiped away, and the symphonies we missed and sunsets we didn't see will be beautifully played over again and again!

The child lost to disease will rush to greet you. The health that eluded you in the winter of your life will return a thousandfold. The friends and family members who died in the faith will sit next to you, singing in the heavenly choir, forever!

All of this will be ours on the day our Lord comes back, and so much more, because when Jesus began His journey, He continued steadfast all the way to the end. Our Savior finished, in spite of His disciple's kiss of betrayal, His friends running for cover, and His countrymen clamoring for His death.

He is Risen!

We can recall that day at Golgotha. The sky is dark. Two criminals are slowly dying, one on His right and one on His left. Jesus is in the middle, taking a deep breath and speaking His last words. John records Him declaring, "It is finished" (John 19:30). Was this a cry of defeat? By no means! Had it not been for the nails, I dare say that Christ's triumphant fist would have lifted toward the sky. And it is because Jesus rose on the third day that we know He is triumphant and that He will return.

Studying with Joy

Yes, there are certainly tasks in life that can seem arduous. Sometimes, we begin a task, thinking it will be satisfying—only to find it to be rather burdensome. When we are paralyzed by discouragement, feel as though we are lost, and yearn with every bone in our body to quit, we can always know that Jesus finds us, picks us up, and carries us close to His heart forever.

Chronicles includes unique stories and emphases that make it a welcome and often fascinating portion of Holy Scripture. So though at times you may feel bogged down, know that you may continue studying 1 and 2 Chronicles with great joy. You may do so because you know the end of the story. God was merciful; He preserved and delivered His people. The temple was rebuilt. And knowing this makes all the difference in the world!

When a Loved One Is Dying

© iStockphoto.com

The individual deaths of thirty-one people, including Saul, Nadab and Abihu, and Jeroboam, are reported in 1 and 2 Chronicles. Some of these deaths were sudden and violent (e.g., Josiah), while others came at the end of a lengthy illness (e.g., Asa). The most famous gradual death in these books is recorded in 2 Chronicles 26:21, where King Uzziah, who had leprosy, was placed in a separate house and excluded from the Lord's temple. His son Jotham had charge of the palace and governed the people while his father died all alone. Certainly, that could not have been an easy time for either of them.

When considering the situation with Uzziah and Jotham, we may well wonder how *we* should respond when a loved one faces a slow, agonizing death. It is helpful to categorize this suffering and death into three stages: (1) before our loved one's health deteriorates, (2) when death is imminent, and (3) after the death of our loved one.

Stage One

Before Our Loved One's Health Deteriorates. Not long after someone is first diagnosed with a terminal illness, medical, spiritual, emotional, and relational issues become a tangled knot that is difficult to untie. God's moral will is objective, complete, and adequate, as revealed in His Word. Yet, the Bible does not tell us the precise answer to every situation. What it *does* tell us is to acquire wisdom and apply it to decisions. As a Christian committed to doing God's will, you can be assured that He is at work in every decision you make. (We read this, for instance, in Romans 8:28: "And we know that for those who love God all things work together for good, for those who are called according to His purpose.") This means that when you make the best decision possible, you can trust Him to work out the results for your family's good and His glory.

It is important to structure all decisions in such a way that there is a shared conversation between the patient's doctors, caregivers, family, and pastor. To help you reach faithful decisions for your loved one, God has placed you into the fellowship of the baptized so that you may seek the counsel of mature believers. Consider Proverbs 15:22: "Without counsel plans fail, but with many advisers they succeed."

Decisions regarding the care of the terminally ill are often fraught with emotion. To urge that we "not be emotional" when it comes to such situations is to oversimplify the problem. It's not that we should be without emotion, but rather that we will not want to allow our emotions to run roughshod over our decision-making process. The goal is not to squelch our feelings but to understand them.

The problem, of course, is that our emotions can so easily be fooled. Solomon spoke to those who were quick to react to their emotions: "Whoever is slow to anger has great understanding, but he who has a hasty temper exalts folly" (Proverbs 14:29). The Bible offers no assurance that we will feel good (or to use the catch-phrase, "be at peace") with every decision we make.

There are numerous decisions you will need to make during this stage, but perhaps the most important of those is to be fully present with your loved one. The most anguished cry from Jesus came not from the thorns, the whip, or the nails. His most painful moment came when He was abandoned by His Father. If the sting of death is sin, then the sting of dying is dying alone. A huge concern of many terminally ill patients is how not to die alone. And so your most profound response to suffering is not in *doing*, but in *being* with your loved one.

Although your loved one is still alert, some spiritual truths need to be faced. Affirm the fact that, due to sin, suffering and death are intrinsic to life and are therefore inescapable. Although Christians cherish life—preserve, nurture, and fight for it—suffering is not ours to master, and death is still the final enemy. Bathe all of these conversations in the good news of Jesus' love and victory over death. Assure your loved one of the great Gospel promises that salvation is by grace, through faith, and not by our own works. Read Revelation 21–22 as a way to bring assurance of the free gift of eternal life that is in Christ Jesus our Lord.

Stage Two

When Death Is Imminent. Some patients are conscious at the time of death, but the burden of disease, end-stage congestive heart failure, dementia, or cancer often causes people to be less aware at that time. Ecclesiastes 8:8a states, "No man has power to retain the spirit, or power over the day of death." You and your loved one are now at this point.

However, it is important at this point to understand that being pro-life does not mean avoiding death at all costs. There is nothing in the Bible that binds Christians to pursue futile and excessively burdensome medical treatment. And yet, if the treatment itself carries no excessive burden and if it will benefit the life the patient has, we may choose it.

The patient will require much support at the time of death. Telling a loved one that it is all right for him to die is appropriate. Repeating this affirmation many times may be necessary, as some patients are afraid to die lest they disappoint someone close to them. They may need to be told to relax and stop struggling; then they can rest and commit themselves to the Lord. Suffering and death are real but not ultimate. They do not speak the last word about the human condition. We may always remember that Jesus has the last word: "I am the resurrection and the life. Whoever believes in Me, though he die, yet shall he live" (John 11:25).

Stage Three

After the Death of Our Loved One. "The Lord gave, and the Lord has taken away" (Job 1:21). Although God did not create us to die, but to live forever in His joyful presence, death is a horrible reality since the fall. It is the enemy we all face at the end of our lives. Death is the awful curse that fell on creation through the sin of Adam and Eve in the Garden of Eden. We cannot gain the victory over death on our own. We need Jesus.

And Jesus assures us that death for the baptized is not extinction, nor is it annihilation. He has conquered death and the grave. Commit your loved one in the sure and certain hope of the resurrection from the dead and a happy reunion in heaven.

For the Christian, death is life's greatest paradox. On the one hand, there is the pain, suffering, and sorrow due to the separation from a loved one. On the other hand, death is a time of thanksgiving for the saint who has gone to be with the Lord. Since there is joy in heaven over one sinner who repents, what a time of celebration there must be when one saint "goes marching in!"

David Prepares for Death

Americans are obsessed with health. We promote health foods, health clubs, healthy diets, and healthy lifestyles. Our consumption of red meat, whole milk, and fatty foods is at an all-time low. Grocery shelves and glossy magazines sport "fat free" this and "lite" that. Smoking is no longer in fashion. We jump and jog, drink purified water, and consume large amounts of vitamins and fiber. Scientific technology has extended our age expectations. Medical breakthroughs stagger our imagination. Yet, we still die; every one of us.

David planned accordingly. We see some of his planning in 1 Chronicles 28:11–18, which details the layout for the temple that his son Solomon was to build. David told him, "All this He made clear to me in writing from the hand of the Lord, all the work to be done according to the plan" (v. 19). David had provided for his nation and family; then "he died at a good age, full of days, riches, and honor" (1 Chronicles 29:28).

One recent study found that most elderly people were sick with their fatal condition three years before their death. Those final years may be filled with grueling medical treatment, but they also afford the opportunity to prepare for death. With the understanding that many people will have this opportunity, we can look to David's greatest Son, Jesus, and also learn from Him to die well. His seven words from the cross teach us what it means to prepare for a good death.

Clockwise: © iStockphoto.com; © Shutterstock, Inc.; © Grady Reese/iStockphoto.com; © Ni Qin/iStockphoto.com; © Fred Froese/iStockphoto.com

Words from the Cross

"Father, forgive them" (Luke 23:34). People often say they want to die suddenly. Yet, quick deaths leave many life tasks incomplete. In contrast to an abrupt and easy death, dying of a progressive illness offers precious opportunities to complete some of life's most important relationships. And often, relationships cannot be completed without the offer and reception of forgiveness.

A proper preparation for death, therefore, means that grudges, bitterness, and anger are placed aside. We are empowered by the Holy Spirit to seek forgiveness from those we have hurt, even as we forgive those who have hurt us. Paul puts it this way: "Be kind to one another, tenderhearted, forgiving one another, as God in Christ forgave you" (Ephesians 4:32).

"Today you will be with Me in Paradise" (Luke 23:43). Jesus promises the malefactor on the cross that they will be reunited in paradise. This is a tremendous encouragement to all who face death. Having faith in Christ's finished work on the cross offers comfort at a time when thoughts of the life to come are especially relevant.

"Behold, your mother!" (John 19:27). According to a national survey, Americans are more likely to talk to their children about drugs and sex than about how they want to die. Discussion of death and dying is nonexistent in most homes. We are inhibited in raising the subject because of fear and discomfort.

But Jesus faced death head-on and attended to what He desired for after He would be deceased. He wanted his beloved disciple John to attend to the care of Mary, His mother.

It is very important to wrap up familial obligations before the time of death. And this means we need to discuss with our loved ones issues revolving around our departure from this life. Setting your house in order applies not only to the physical and financial welfare of your family, but also to their spiritual welfare as it pertains to their Christian lives.

"Why have You forsaken Me?" (Mark 15:34). In His cry of abandonment, Jesus carried a burden that none of us ever will: the sins of the world. We will never know full communion with God only to have it cut off. Yet, for a person receiving the diagnosis of a terminal illness, it can seem as if God is absent, as if he or she has been abandoned. Jesus acknowledged this feeling as well, but in doing so He showed us how to work through despair. Honestly dealing with God, even when we feel forsaken by Him, is all important.

"I thirst" (John 19:28). Jesus not only experienced spiritual grief, but He also felt physical anguish. When we are incurably sick, we may worry about being a burden on others, and we may be bothered by the "indignity" of needing help with the most basic tasks: dressing, eating, and bathing. Yet, in an age where death often comes after years of decreasing health, we must learn that dignity does not come from being able to button a shirt or cook a meal. This is one thing we may learn from Jesus in His vulnerable moment of thirst. After this cry, He was given some sour wine, and rather than rejecting it, He drank the gift.

"It is finished" (John 19:30). Those who work with the dying often report being amazed with how long a dying person can cling to life. And then, when a birthday, a visit from a family member, or another important event passes, the dying person quickly lets go. Jesus' first five words show us how to *prepare* to die. At the end, Jesus shows us *how* to die. Recognizing that His life is complete, Jesus says, "It is finished."

Upon making amends with family and friends, being assured that "the free gift of God is eternal life in Christ Jesus our Lord" (Romans 6:23b), putting our house in order, honestly lamenting our suffering, and embracing our physical limitations, we will be able to declare, "It is finished." We may die in the confidence that not only is Jesus the Author of our Christian life in Baptism, but He will also now be its Perfecter.

"Father, into Your hands I commit My spirit!" (Luke 23:46). There is a time to be born and a time to die. Our Lord's final words show us that in death we commend ourselves to the Father, who placed His name upon us in Baptism, who often nourished us with our Savior's true body and blood, who throughout our lives absolved us of our sins, and who repeatedly spoke to us words that "our Savior Christ Jesus . . . abolished death and brought life and immortality to light through the Gospel" (2 Timothy 1:10). It is *this* loving heavenly Father to whom we say, "Father, into Your hands I commit my spirit."

Words for Eternity

It is true: for as long as this present world stands, like David, we will all have to face death. This can indeed be an overwhelming thing to contemplate.

The last words of Jesus *from* the cross provide a great model and comfort, but it is finally the work of Christ *on* the cross that has transformed death from a defeated end to a glorious beginning. Death for the baptized is an enemy, but through Christ it is a defeated enemy. It is in the control of our loving Father. And so with the psalmist we may say, "Precious in the sight of the LORD is the death of His saints" (Psalm 116:15).

ACCESS: Solomon Dedicates the Temple

Imagine a person walking in front of the White House, seeking access to the President of the United States. Better yet, imagine that person is you.

There you are in fine form. Your shoes are shined, your hair is combed, and you are dressed in your Sunday best. You want an audience with the Commander-in-Chief because there are some burning issues you must take up with him. First, there is the problem of the new highway in town. It doesn't have an exit ramp close enough to your home. And then there's the issue of income taxes. They are too high for you and too low for everybody else. Finally, there is that sticky matter called your mortgage. Couldn't the president make a few phone calls and get you off the hook? But, let's be honest. There are far too many barriers between you and the president. The gates are locked. The guards won't let you in. His staff doesn't know your name. And the Secret Service has orders to shoot first and ask questions later. Sure, it's fun to fantasize about sharing your hurts and hopes with the most powerful person on the planet. But it's just not going to happen.

Let's face it. Far too often, we don't have the right connections with the right person at the right time to accomplish all the right things. If we could just get access!

But what if the president looks out his window on Pennsylvania Avenue and sees you? What if he gives the command and his security detail escorts you right into the Oval Office? And what if the president attentively listens and makes all the changes you ask for? Would that be too good to be true? With the President of the United States, perhaps. But with the King of the Universe, we have a Friend in high places.

Solomon's Greatest Achievement

The greatest of Solomon's accomplishments was building the temple in Jerusalem. The previous center of worship had been the tabernacle, set up in Shiloh to the north of Jerusalem. Now the Lord allowed Solomon to construct a more permanent place for Him to dwell on earth. With the help of 180,000 laborers, the temple was completed in seven years.

Although the Lord is so great that heaven and the highest heaven cannot contain Him, His name takes up residence in Solomon's temple. "Name," referring to God's name, is mentioned fourteen times in 2 Chronicles 6. A name in Hebrew represents the person who bears it; hence, where God's name is, there He is present. To confirm that the Lord was truly present, we have these words: "As soon as Solomon finished his prayer, fire came down from heaven and consumed the burnt offering and the sacrifices, and the glory of the Lord filled the temple" (2 Chronicles 7:1).

Israel was commanded to pray nowhere else but toward the Lord's dwelling place, which He had chosen and designated. In Exodus 20:24, the Lord puts it this way: "In every place where I cause My name to be remembered I will come to you and bless you."

Portions of this article originally appeared on ConcordiaTheology.org.

Separated from Holiness

Normally, the Old Testament describes the Lord as dwelling in Israel's tabernacle, Solomon's temple, in the city of Jerusalem, or on Mount Zion. The Scriptures, however, also assert that God dwells in eternity; this is as far away from planet earth as possible. The Lord is revealed to us in the Bible as being the absolute, infinite, eternal, all-powerful, all-knowing, and only God. In Isaiah 40, the prophet says that the Lord sits above the circle of the earth and from there we look like grasshoppers in His eyes. Isaiah also says there that whole nations before Him are like a drop in a bucket, as dust on a scale. Seraphim in Isaiah 6 cover their faces and their feet as they continually cry out before Him, "Holy, holy, holy!"

It is no wonder, then, that the prophets state that both the Lord's *name* and His *place* are holy. They are unique, separate, different, and completely removed. Isaiah, for instance, employs the word "holy" sixty-nine times in his book, and nineteen times he refers to the Lord as "the Holy One of Israel." We, on the other hand, are sinful. Obviously, this means that there are massive barriers between God and us. The gates are locked. The hosts of heaven will not let us in. All who are sinful and unclean must stay out.

Yet, Isaiah 57:15 goes on to assert that the Lord dwells "with him who is of a contrite and lowly spirit." I know what you are thinking: "If I can just get really contrite and really lowly, I'll gain access to the Lord." Good luck with that. We will never be contrite and lowly enough. You see, we are intoxicated with just the opposite. The Bible calls it pride.

The Mother of All Sins

At the dedication of the temple, in 2 Chronicles 6, Solomon knelt before the assembly and spread his hands toward heaven. He urged people to confess their sins, and he even stated that non-Israelites have access to the Lord. Throughout this prayer, Solomon indicated that God hears the prayers of the humble, while pride blocks access to the Lord's presence. All throughout the Scriptures, we read that the Lord is against every form of pride.

> *[He is] against all that is lifted up—and it shall be brought low; against all the cedars of Lebanon, lofty and lifted up; and against all the oaks of Bashan; against all the lofty mountains, and against all the uplifted hills; against every high tower, and against every fortified wall; against all the ships of Tarshish, and against all the beautiful craft. And the haughtiness of man shall be humbled, and the lofty pride of men shall be brought low, and the LORD alone will be exalted in that day. (Isaiah 2:12–17)*

Twice in this poem, we are told that the Lord alone will be lifted up on that day. The High and Lofty One tolerates no rivals.

Gregory the Great (c. 540–604) said that pride is the mother of all sins. Medieval artists depicted pride as a peacock walking around, arrogantly strutting its stuff. Pride was portrayed by Milton in *Paradise Lost* with these damning words: "Better to reign in hell, than to serve in heaven." And Luther's dictum was "all sin is pride."

Pride refuses to utter the three toughest words in the English language: "I was wrong." Or the four hardest words: "I am not perfect." Or the five most painful words: "I guess you are right." Or the six most difficult words: "I think I need some help."

Because pride lurks in every human heart, we may feel as though we will never gain access to our God. But the good news is this: there is someone who is absolutely and totally humble. *And He is our access.*

Like a Lamb That Is Led to the Slaughter

In Isaiah 53:2, the prophet writes, "For He grew up before Him like a young plant, and like a root out of dry ground; He had no form or majesty that we should look at Him, and no beauty that we should desire Him." Later in that same chapter, Isaiah goes on to describe Jesus as a humble Lamb led to the slaughter.

One night, the disciples were fast asleep, and the next minute they were fast afoot. The next morning, the Jews just wanted Barabbas, and the soldiers just wanted to have some fun. Herod wanted a show, while Pilate simply wanted out. Caiaphas wanted death. And what about the executioners? All they wanted was Jesus' blood.

Their strategy was singular: beat Him within an inch of death and then stop. His back was lacerated by lashes, but they shoved the crossbeam on it. When He came to the Place of the Skull, they nailed Him to wood. And there He hung, completely crushed by the sin of all people.

The Father's plan was to offer Jesus not only as our sin-bearer, but also as our death-destroyer. Raised from the dead and seated at the Father's right hand, Jesus is now our access to the throne of grace. Indeed, Hebrews 10:19 states, "Therefore, brothers . . . we have confidence to enter the holy places by the blood of Jesus."

Imagine that! By the blood of Jesus, we have access into the Most Holy Place of the Most Holy God who has the Most Holy name! In Jesus Christ, we finally have the right connections with the right person at the right time to accomplish all the right things for the glory and honor of our God!

One Greater than Solomon

So why remain outside, alone, feeling as though you have no access to the most powerful person in the universe?

Because you do! The barriers are down and the gates are unlocked. One greater than Solomon is here! His name is Jesus, and He is our way to the Father, as He tells us Himself: "No one comes to the Father except through Me" (John 14:6).

Humble, Pray, Seek, and Turn

© Michael Utech/iStockphoto.com

Some of the things that we have to face in life can hit us like an earthquake. You know the feeling, and so do I. Satan, our spiritual enemy, whispers in our ear, and his temptations are sometimes very attractive. We give in, and the next day we feel dirty and consumed with guilt.

Or maybe the sin of parents or grandparents continues to rattle your world. Alcohol, abuse, or abandonment have left their scars on your heart and in your home. And, try as you might, you just can't shake the feelings of worthlessness and shame. If you face the enemy's fiery accusations or have a huge hole in your heart because of family dysfunction, then take heart. We can learn from several kings in 2 Chronicles who experienced this type of pain. Some had to face deadly enemies, while others had to work through the mess left by their fathers.

Learning from the Kings

In the first category is Asa, who met Zerah the Cushite and his vast army, as well as Jehoshaphat who, for his part, had to face a daunting coalition consisting of Moabites, Ammonites, and Meunites. In the second category is Hezekiah, whose reign began with an idolatrous monstrosity left by his father, Ahaz; also in this category is Josiah, who was met with the rampant idolatry left over from the reigns of his grandfather Manasseh and his father, Amon.

Against innumerable odds, these kings survived and even thrived. Their faith intersected with the Lord's promises in 2 Chronicles 7:14: "If My people who are called by My name humble themselves, and pray and seek My face and turn from their wicked ways, then I will hear from heaven and will forgive their sin and heal their land."

Using 2 Chronicles 7:14, we may outline the lives of these kings as follows:

The King	*His Place in 2 Chronicles*	*Summary of His Reign*
Asa	2 Chronicles 14–16	Seek the Lord
Jehoshaphat	2 Chronicles 17–20	Pray to the Lord
Hezekiah	2 Chronicles 29–32	Turn to the Lord
Josiah	2 Chronicles 34–35	Be humble before the Lord

When these Southern kings felt their entire world collapsing around them, God promised to hear their cries, forgive their sins, and heal their land. Asa, Jehoshaphat, Hezekiah, and Josiah point us to Judah's greatest king, whose life and love guarantee that the promises in 2 Chronicles 7:14 are also for us.

Relying on the Greatest King

When everything cracks and crumbles, when our world shatters all around us, when Satan attacks our faith, and when all our dreams become our worst nightmares, Jesus redeems, rescues, and restores us.

But how can we know this for sure?

Let's go back in time when, one night, it all began with a few small tremors. In fact, they were so small no one even noticed. But then the shaking picked up when the treasurer left the room.

Within minutes, these tremors increased in their intensity. And in staccato-like fashion, massive earthquakes began to hit: One kiss, three nails, and six hours of crying out under the sin of the world. Jesus finally collapsed under the weight of it all. And then there was a huge earthquake: "And behold, the curtain of the temple was torn in two, from top to bottom. And the earth shook, and the rocks were split" (Matthew 27:51).

But in Matthew 28:2, the evangelist records another earthquake, even more massive: "And behold, there was a great earthquake, for an angel of the Lord descended from heaven and came and rolled back the stone and sat on it." And then what the angel said unleashed the greatest news the world has ever heard: "He is not here, for He has risen, as He said" (v. 6). This news has continued to change the world ever since!

In Christ's death, we find promises that heal the hurts inflicted by others and protection from Satan's accusations. To guarantee it, Jesus left us words of love: "and He took bread, and when He had given thanks, He broke it and gave it to them, saying, 'This is My body, which is given for you. Do this in remembrance of Me.' And likewise the cup after they had eaten, saying, 'This cup that is poured out for you is the new covenant in My blood'" (Luke 22:19–20). In this Holy Supper, Jesus gives us victory over the devil and his lies, and also hope for the wounds in our lives. The very gates of hell will never, ever prevail against His resurrection victory.

The Kings in Detail

All four of the kings that we listed above faced some difficult, earthquake-like troubles during their reigns over the Southern Kingdom of Judah. Over the next several articles, we will be looking at the themes in 2 Chronicles 7:14 to learn how Asa, Jehoshaphat, Hezekiah, and Josiah withstood earthquake-like disasters in their lives.

In doing so, we will learn about seeking the Lord, praying to Him, turning to Him, and being humble. Through it all, we will get glimpses of Jesus, our perfect King and only Savior.

Study Guide

Cover art: King Solomon, by Maestro de Becerril, c. 1525. Fine Art Images/Fine Art Images

LifeLight Expands

LifeLight

Available NOW!

The Bible: An Overview
Genesis, Pt. 1
Genesis, Pt. 2
Exodus, Pt. 1
Exodus, Pt. 2
Wilderness Wanderings
Joshua
Judges
Ruth/Esther
1 & 2 Samuel
Life of David
1 & 2 Kings
1 & 2 Chronicles
Ezra/Nehemiah
Job
Selected Psalms
Proverbs
Ecclesiastes/Song of Solomon
Isaiah, Pt. 1
Isaiah, Pt. 2
Daniel
Hosea/Joel/Amos
Minor Prophets
Nahum/Habakkuk/Zephaniah
Haggai/Zechariah/Malachi
Matthew, Pt. 1
Matthew, Pt. 2
Mark
Luke, Pt. 1
Luke, Pt. 2
John, Pt. 1
John, Pt. 2
Acts, Pt. 1
Acts, Pt. 2
Romans, Pt. 1
Romans, Pt. 2
1 Corinthians
2 Corinthians
Galatians/Philippians/Colossians
Ephesians/1 & 2 Thessalonians
Timothy/Titus/Philemon
Hebrews
James/Jude
1 & 2 Peter
1, 2, 3 John
Revelation

LifeLight Foundations

Baptism
Bible Feasts
Creation, New Creation
The Christian's Mission
End Times
Heaven & Hell
Law & Gospel
Ministry
Miracles
Parables
Prayer
Prophecy
Triune God
Worship

LifeLight Release Schedule

2015 RELEASES

LifeLight—Jeremiah/Lamentations	January
LifeLight—Ezekiel	April
LifeLight—Obadiah/Jonah/Micah	July

I Will Build the House
1 Chronicles 1–12

Distribute before session 1 for use in session 1.
Use enrichment magazine pp. 2–4.

Resources for Worship

Use these resources for your daily study at home and at the week's assembly.

Hymn

Jerusalem the golden,
With milk and honey blest—
The promise of salvation,
The place of peace and rest—
We know not, oh, we know not
What joys await us there:
The radiancy of glory,
The bliss beyond compare!

Within those walls of Zion
Sounds forth the joyful song,
As saints join with the angels
And all the martyr throng.
The Prince is ever with them;
The daylight is serene;
The city of the blessèd
Shines bright with glorious sheen.

Around the throne of David,
The saints, from care released,
Raise loud their songs of triumph
To celebrate the feast.
They sing to Christ their leader,
Who conquered in the fight,
Who won for them forever
Their gleaming robes of white.

O sweet and blessèd country,
The home of God's elect!
O sweet and blessèd country
That faithful hearts expect!
In mercy, Jesus, bring us
To that eternal rest
With You and God the Father
And Spirit, ever blest.

LSB 672

Prayer

O God, You made of one blood all nations of men who dwell on the face of the earth. To encourage all, You sent your only-begotten Son, the Son of David, for our salvation; grant that all the peoples of the world may seek Your mercy in Jesus Christ and receive Your indwelling Spirit. Hasten, O heavenly Father, the fulfillment of Your promises of an everlasting kingdom; through Jesus Christ, our Savior, we pray. Amen.

Digging Deep
My Personal Study for Week 1

Day 1 • Read Ezra 3:8–13; 1 Chronicles 1; 9:1–34

1. The two books we call 1 and 2 Chronicles were originally written as one long account. Later, they were divided into two parts, or "books," as we call them today. Based on 1 Chronicles 9:1–34, for whom was Chronicles written?

2. Read Ezra 3:8–13.

a. What momentous events occurred in the generations before the Chronicles were written?

b. How were people feeling about these events?

3. Based on the first word in Chronicles, what is the scope of the Chronicler's history?

4. What does the scope of the Chronicler's writing tell us about the importance of his message?

Day 2 • Read 1 Chronicles 2:1–4:23

5. Based on 1 Chronicles 2:1–4, what will be the focus of the Chronicler's genealogy?

6. Genealogy not only sums up family history, but it also connects us to broader history. See 1 Chronicles 2:5–50, which refers to a number of important Bible characters. Write below a summary of what you know about some of these characters. (Look up the passages if you need help.)

a. Achan (Joshua 7)

b. Boaz (Ruth 4)

c. Jesse (1 Samuel 16)

d. Caleb (Joshua 14:6–15)

Day 3 • Read 1 Chronicles 6

7. What were the three clans of the Levites?

8. According to 6:31–32, 48, how did these clans serve? (You will read more about them later in Chronicles.)

9. How was the service of Aaron and his sons different from that of other Levites?

The Cornerstone of the House
1 Chronicles 13–20

Distribute before session 2 for use in session 2.
Use enrichment magazine pp. 5–7.

Resources for Worship

Use these resources for your daily study at home and at the week's assembly.

Hymn

Fight the good fight with all your might;
Christ is your strength, and Christ your right.
Lay hold on life, and it shall be
Your joy and crown eternally.

Run the straight race through God's good grace;
Lift up your eyes, and seek His face.
Life with its way before us lies;
Christ is the path, and Christ the prize.

Cast care aside, lean on your guide;
His boundless mercy will provide.
Trust, and enduring faith shall prove
Christ is your life and Christ your love.

Faint not nor fear, His arms are near;
He changes not who holds you dear;
Only believe, and you will see
That Christ is all eternally.

LSB 664

Prayer

Almighty God, You chose David as the instrument of Your reign in Israel. Grant that the kingdom of David's Son, Jesus, may set us free from the bondage of sin and establish our hearts in peace and faithful worship; through Jesus Christ, Your Son, our Lord, who lives and reigns with You and the Holy Spirit, one God, now and forever. Amen.

Digging Deep
My Personal Study for Week 2

Day 1 • Read 1 Chronicles 13–14

1. According to 1 Samuel 4:10–11; 6:21–7:2, how did the ark of the covenant, the most precious religious object in Israel, end up at Kiriath-jearim?

2. How did David go about bringing the ark toward Jerusalem, according to 1 Chronicles 13:1–4?

3. The ark of God is described in 13:6. What does this description say about God's relationship to Israel?

4. Why had the Lord "broken out" against Uzzah the priest? (Cf. Exodus 25:12–15.)

5. The king of Tyre and the Philistines reacted very differently to the news of David's reign. Contrast their reactions below.

Day 2 • Read 1 Chronicles 15

6. How was the procession with the ark of the covenant different this time from the episode in chapter 13?

7. David urged the priests and Levites to make special preparations for moving the ark. According to Exodus 19:10, 14–15, how were such preparations made?

8. How is such preparation different for believers today, according to Hebrews 10:19–24?

9. Characterize below the procession with the ark, based on 1 Chronicles 15:16–28.

10. *For personal reflection. Sharing optional.* What lessons would you draw from this account for the following:

a. Yourself

b. Your congregation

c. Your nation

Day 3 • Read 1 Chronicles 16

11. **Challenge question.** David appointed a song of thanksgiving for the moving of the ark. Portions of the song are comparable with portions of other psalms (e.g., briefly compare 16:8–22 with Psalm 105:1–15; 16:23–33 with Psalm 96; and 16:34–36 with Psalm 106:1, 48). What can this tell us about psalms in ancient Israel?

12. What mission does the song begin with (16:8–9)?

13. a. In verses 14–22, David gives Israel a history lesson. What history did he present?

Preparations for the House

1 Chronicles 21–27

Distribute before session 3 for use in session 3.
Use enrichment magazine pp. 8–10.

Resources for Worship

Use these resources for your daily study at home and at the week's assembly.

Hymn

I love Your kingdom, Lord,
The place of Your abode,
The Church our blest Redeemer saved
With His own precious blood.

Beyond my highest joy
I prize its heav'nly ways,
Its sweet communion, solemn vows,
Its hymns of love and praise.

I love Your Church, O God,
Your saints in ev'ry land,
Dear as the apple of Your eye
And graven on Your hand.

For them my tears shall fall;
For them my prayers ascend;
For them my cares and toils be giv'n
Till toils and cares shall end.

Sure as Your truth shall last,
To Zion shall be giv'n
The brightest glories earth can yield
And brighter bliss of heav'n.

LSB 651

Prayer

Grant us, Lord, Your Holy Spirit, so that our minds and deeds bring honor to Your name. May we confess Your goodness through our lives and serve others according to Your gracious will; through Jesus Christ, Your Son, our Lord, who lives and reigns with You and the Holy Spirit, one God, now and forever. Amen.

Digging Deep
My Personal Study for Week 3

Day 1 • Read 1 Chronicles 21

1. a. Who incited David to action?

b. What action did David take?

2. Why would this displease the Lord?

3. When the Lord's prophet Gad invited David to choose a punishment, how did David respond?

4. *For personal reflection. Sharing optional.* Read David's prayer in 21:17. If your decisions have harmed others, how would you pray about that?

5. a. What means did the Lord provide to David for reconciling with Him?

b. What means has God provided for your reconciliation?

Day 2 • Read 1 Chronicles 22

6. According to 22:1, what unexpected outcome resulted from David's sin over the census?

7. **Challenge question.**

a. Compare David's activities and decisions with the circumstances of 1 Kings 1:5–13. What significant event has the Chronicler omitted?

b. Why might the Chronicler, writing for the returned exiles, omit this event?

8. Why was David not allowed to build the temple?

9. What does this say about the Lord?

In chapter 22, the Lord gave David a key promise, saying, "Behold, a son shall be born to you who shall be a man of rest. I will give him rest from all his surrounding enemies. For his name shall be Solomon, and I will give peace and quiet to Israel in his days. He shall build a house for My name. He shall be My son, and I will be his father, and I will establish his royal throne in Israel forever."

Day 3 • Read 1 Chronicles 23

10. a. According to Numbers 4:1–3; 8:23–24, at what ages were Levites considered eligible to minister?

b. Based on 1 Chronicles 23:24–27, how did David adjust the age further?

11. What reasons did David give for changing the service of the Levites in 23:25–26?

The House Is Built

1 Chronicles 28–2 Chronicles 4

Distribute before session 4 for use in session 4.
Use enrichment magazine pp. 11–13.

Resources for Worship

Use these resources for your daily study at home and at the week's assembly.

Hymn

Baptized into Your name most holy,
O Father, Son, and Holy Ghost,
I claim a place, though weak and lowly,
Among Your saints, Your chosen host.
Buried with Christ and dead to sin,
Your Spirit now shall live within.

My loving Father, here You take me
To be henceforth Your child and heir.
My faithful Savior, here You make me
The fruit of all Your sorrows share.
O Holy Spirit, comfort me
When threat'ning clouds around I see.

My faithful God, You fail me never;
Your promise surely will endure.
O cast me not away forever
If words and deeds become impure.
Have mercy when I come defiled;
Forgive, lift up, restore Your child.

All that I am and love most dearly—
Receive it all, O Lord, from me.
Let me confess my faith sincerely;
Help me Your faithful child to be!
Let nothing that I am or own
Serve any will but Yours alone.

LSB 590

Prayer

Dearest Lord Jesus Christ, to redeem us from our sins, You endured the cross and overcame death by the miracle of Your resurrection. Deliver us from those who oppose us and the work of Your kingdom. Grant that we may, through daily contrition and repentance, be rid of our sins and arise in new life through Your life-giving Spirit; for You live and reign with the Father and the Holy Spirit, one God, now and forever. Amen.

Digging Deep
My Personal Study for Week 4

Day 1 • Read 1 Chronicles 28

1. According to David's speech to Israel, on what is the kingdom founded?

2. How will the Lord establish Solomon as king?

3. a. What must Israel seek, according to David?

b. Apply this in your own life. What is God charging you to do as you seek Him?

4. According to 28:9–10, what is God like?

5. With what words of encouragement and promises did David hand over the work of the kingdom to Solomon?

The Lord said to Joshua before the conquest, "This Book of the Law shall not depart from your mouth, but you shall meditate on it day and night, so that you may be careful to do according to all that is written in it. For then you will make your way prosperous, and then you will have good success. Have I not commanded you? Be strong and courageous. Do not be frightened, and do not be dismayed, for the LORD your God is with you wherever you go" (Joshua 1:8–9).

Day 2 • Read 1 Chronicles 29

6. For what reasons did David work to prepare for the building of the temple, according to 29:1–5?

7. a. What characterized the offerings of the people?

b. *For personal reflection. Sharing optional.* How does this speak to you about your offerings at church and to other godly causes?

8. **Challenge question.** The traditional doxology for the Lord's Prayer is likely based on 1 Chronicles 29:11, which states, "Yours, O LORD, is the greatness and the power and the glory and the victory and the majesty, for all that is in the heavens and in the earth is Yours. Yours is the kingdom, O LORD, and You are exalted as head above all." How is this Old Testament doxology a fitting conclusion to the prayer Jesus taught us?

9. a. According to David's prayer, in what does God take pleasure?

b. Why is this a source of pleasure to God?

Jesus said, "Seek His kingdom. . . . Fear not, little flock, for it is your Father's good pleasure to give you the kingdom" (Luke 12:31–32).

Day 3 • Read 2 Chronicles 1–2

10. Why did Solomon gather all Israel at Gibeon?

11. What offer did God make to Solomon that night?

The Lord Enters His House

2 Chronicles 5–9

Distribute before session 5 for use in session 5.
Use enrichment magazine pp. 14–16.

Resources for Worship

Use these resources for your daily study at home and at the week's assembly.

Hymn

The Church's one foundation
Is Jesus Christ, her Lord;
She is His new creation
By water and the Word.
From heav'n He came and sought her
To be His holy bride;
With His own blood He bought her,
And for her life He died.

Elect from ev'ry nation,
Yet one o'er all the earth;
Her charter of salvation:
One Lord, one faith, one birth.
One holy name she blesses,
Partakes one holy food,
And to one hope she presses
With ev'ry grace endued.

Though with a scornful wonder
The world sees her oppressed,
By schisms rent asunder,
By heresies distressed,
Yet saints their watch are keeping;
Their cry goes up, "How long?"
And soon the night of weeping
Shall be the morn of song.

Through toil and tribulation
And tumult of her war
She waits the consummation
Of peace forevermore
Till with the vision glorious
Her longing eyes are blest,
And the great Church victorious
Shall be the Church at rest.

Yet she on earth has union
With God, the Three in One,
And mystic sweet communion
With those whose rest is won.
O blessèd heav'nly chorus!
Lord, save us by Your grace
That we, like saints before us,
May see You face to face.

LSB 644

Prayer

Glorious Lord, whose presence filled the temple and whose wisdom filled the heart and mind of King Solomon, grant us this day Your Holy Spirit and His wisdom so that we may spread Your reign to our neighbors and the nations, filling them with joy in Christ Jesus, who lives and reigns with You and the Holy Spirit, one God, now and forever. Amen.

Digging Deep
My Personal Study for Week 5

Day 1 • Read 2 Chronicles 5:1–6:11

1. Chapter 5 is a reprise of earlier events. What thematic event is presented again?

2. a. What feast is described in Leviticus 23:33–43?

b. How were the events of 2 Chronicles 5 appropriate to this feast?

3. What does the detail of 5:9 tell us about the antiquity of the Chronicler's report?

4. What significance does the cloud have in the day's events?

5. a. According to 5:10 and 6:11, what was in the ark?

b. What does this say about the enduring significance of the contents also for our lives?

Day 2 • Read 2 Chronicles 6:12–42

6. a. What gestures did Solomon use as he prayed?

b. What is the significance of such gestures?

7. According to Solomon, how has the Lord distinguished Himself from the gods of the nations?

8. How did Solomon describe God's presence in 6:18–21?

9. What was the purpose of the temple, according to 6:22–31?

10. How did Israel carry out God's mission in the Old Testament, according to 6:32–33?

Rebellion in the House, Part 1

2 Chronicles 10–16

Distribute before session 6 for use in session 6.
Use enrichment magazine pp. 17–19.

Resources for Worship

Use these resources for your daily study at home and at the week's assembly.

Hymn

Spread the reign of God the Lord,
Spoken, written, mighty Word;
Ev'rywhere His creatures call
To His heav'nly banquet hall.

Tell how God the Father's will
Made the world, upholds it still,
How His own dear Son He gave
Us from sin and death to save.

Tell of our Redeemer's grace,
Who, to save our human race
And to pay rebellion's price,
Gave Himself as sacrifice.

Tell of God the Spirit giv'n
Now to guide us on to heav'n,
Strong and holy, just and true,
Working both to will and do.

Enter, mighty Word, the field;
Ripe the promise of its yield.
But the reapers, oh, how few
For the work there is to do!

Lord of harvest, great and kind,
Rouse to action heart and mind;
Let the gath'ring nations all
See Your light and heed Your call

LSB 830

Prayer

Merciful Father, You have made known to us Your gracious good will in the gift of Your Son, Jesus, who bore our sins and suffering upon the cross. Lead us by faith to show mercy toward others, no matter what circumstances of life surround us; through Your Son, Jesus Christ, who lives and reigns with You and the Holy Spirit, one God, now and forever. Amen.

Digging Deep
My Personal Study for Week 6

Day 1 • Read 2 Chronicles 10:1–11:12

1. The story of Rehoboam's accession to the throne is filled with political intrigue. Based on 10:1–11, who were the main players?

2. Write below what each person or group was looking for in the new administration.

3. According to Ahijah the Shilonite, what was the ultimate reason for Rehoboam's decisions in this matter?

4. How do the words of Shemaiah the man of God affirm the words of Ahijah?

5. What steps did Rehoboam take to maintain control over the tribes of Judah and Benjamin?

Day 2 • Read 2 Chronicles 11:13–12:16

6. A migration is described in 2 Chronicles 11:12–17. What physical and spiritual causes motivated this migration?

Physical

Spiritual

7. Compare 1 Kings 11:1–8 with 2 Chronicles 11:18–21. How did the reign of Rehoboam reflect the reign of his father, Solomon?

8. What shrewd actions did Rehoboam take, according to 2 Chronicles 11:22–33?

9. How did the Lord respond to Rehoboam's decision to abandon the Law of the Lord?

10. **Challenge question.** What good spiritual counsel can we derive for our lives from the story of Rehoboam?

Day 3 • Read 2 Chronicles 13

11. What military challenges did Abijah face when he invaded the hill country of Ephraim?

12. Summarize the main point of Abijah's speech (13:4–12).

Rebellion in the House, Part 2

2 Chronicles 17–22

Distribute before session 7 for use in session 7.
Use enrichment magazine pp. 20–22.

Resources for Worship

Use these resources for your daily study at home and at the week's assembly.

Hymn

Sing praise to God, the highest good,
The author of creation,
The God of love who understood
Our need for His salvation.
With healing balm our souls He fills
And ev'ry faithless murmur stills:
To God all praise and glory!

What God's almighty pow'r has made,
In mercy He is keeping.
By morning glow or evening shade
His eye is never sleeping.
Within the kingdom of His might
All things are just and good and right:
To God all praise and glory!

We sought the Lord in our distress;
O God, in mercy hear us.
Our Savior saw our helplessness
And came with peace to cheer us.
For this we thank and praise the Lord,
Who is by one and all adored:
To God all praise and glory!

He never shall forsake His flock,
His chosen generation;
He is their refuge and their rock,
Their peace and their salvation.
As with a mother's tender hand,
He leads His own, His chosen band:
To God all praise and glory!

All who confess Christ's holy name,
Give God the praise and glory.
Let all who know His pow'r proclaim
Aloud the wondrous story.
Cast ev'ry idol from its throne,
For God is God, and He alone:
To God all praise and glory!

LSB 819

Prayer

O Lord, the fount of Your mercy never runs dry. Pour Your mercy upon us and cleanse us from our sins, so that we may stand ready to serve You and one another. And because Your Church cannot abide without Your aid, grant her faithful leaders and devoted servants; for You live and reign with the Father and the Holy Spirit, one God, now and forever. Amen.

Digging Deep
My Personal Study for Week 7

Day 1 • Read 2 Chronicles 17

1. Compare 2 Chronicles 14:1–8 with 17:1–6. Note below similarities between Jehoshaphat and Asa, his father.

2. What lessons for parenthood or family life might you draw from the answers to question 1?

3. Describe the teaching mission initiated by Jehoshaphat.

Scope of the mission

Content of the mission

Teachers for the mission

4. What examples of success attended Jehoshaphat's early reign?

Day 2 • Read 2 Chronicles 18:1–22

5. What kind of alliance existed between Israel and Judah?

6. How did Jehoshaphat show himself to be a godly king in his decision making?

7. Micaiah prophesied three times to Ahab about his decision to fight the Syrians. Why do the prophecies grow progressively more ominous?

8. Compare Numbers 23:19 with 2 Chronicles 18:19–21. What truths about the Lord do these passages teach?

9. What principles of right and wrong may the children of God draw for themselves from the Lord's example in these passages from Numbers and 2 Chronicles?

Day 3 • Read 2 Chronicles 18:23–19:11

10. Despite faithfully speaking God's Word, the prophet Micaiah suffered at the hand of the false prophet Zedekiah and King Ahab. In the face of such suffering, what example does Micaiah leave for us?

Rebellion in the House, Part 3

2 Chronicles 23–28

Distribute before session 8 for use in session 8.
Use enrichment magazine pp. 23–26.

Resources for Worship

Use these resources for your daily study at home and at the week's assembly.

Hymn

Renew me, O eternal Light,
And let my heart and soul be bright,
Illumined with the light of grace
That issues from Your holy face.

Remove the pow'r of sin from me
And cleanse all my impurity
That I may have the strength and will
Temptations of the flesh to still.

Create in me a new heart, Lord,
That gladly I obey Your Word.
Let what You will be my desire,
And with new life my soul inspire.

Grant that I only You may love
And seek those things which are above
Till I behold You face to face,
O Light eternal, through Your grace.

LSB 704

Prayer

Almighty and everlasting Father of our Lord and Savior Jesus Christ, we see and feel how Your Church is doing in this world. We see its status and how it is annoyed in so many ways by the world and the devil. So we pray to You for the sake of Your only-begotten Son. First, comfort and strengthen our hearts by Your Holy Spirit so that we may not be overwhelmed by so many dangers. Also we pray that You will not only halt the purposes and plans of the enemies, but will also truly and marvelously help prove to the whole world that You care for the Church. Rule, protect, and deliver her, ever-living and reigning, eternal God. Amen.

Digging Deep
My Personal Study for Week 8

Day 1 • Read 2 Chronicles 23

1. Jehoiada, the husband of brave Jehoshabeath, is a remarkable figure. What preparations does he take to ensure the survival of the house of David?

2. **Challenge question.** Based on what you have studied thus far in Chronicles, how would you characterize the relationship between the house of David and the tribe of Levi?

3. How does Athaliah's response to the coup dramatically illustrate its effectiveness?

4. Jehoiada introduced a covenant with four parties. List the four parties:

5. How do the parties demonstrate their loyalty under the covenant?

Day 2 • Read 2 Chronicles 24

6. How does the account in Chronicles make clear that Joash was the one who planned for the repairs to the temple, rather than Jehoiada as regent?

7. How was Joash's plan for raising funds similar to and different from the way churches receive offerings today?

8. How did the death of Jehoiada illustrate his importance to the well-being of Judah?

9. a. Who was Zechariah?

b. What was his message to Joash?

10. How did the servants who assassinated Joash show the influence of Jehoiada upon the kingdom of Judah?

Day 3 • Read 2 Chronicles 25

11. How did the actions of Amaziah illustrate that he would follow the Lord, "yet not with a whole heart"?

The House Will Be Rebuilt

2 Chronicles 29–36

Distribute before session 9 for use in session 9.
Use enrichment magazine pp. 27–32.

Resources for Worship

Use these resources for your daily study at home and at the week's assembly.

Hymn

Oh, blest the house, whate'er befall,
Where Jesus Christ is all in all!
A home that is not wholly His—
How sad and poor and dark it is!

Oh, blest that house where faith is found
And all in hope and love abound;
They trust their God and serve Him still
And do in all His holy will!

Oh, blest the parents who give heed
Unto their children's foremost need
And weary not of care or cost.
May none to them and heav'n be lost!

Oh, blest that house; it prospers well.
In peace and joy the parents dwell,
And in their children's lives is shown
How richly God can bless His own.

Then here will I and mine today
A solemn promise make and say:
Though all the world forsake His Word,
I and my house will serve the Lord!

LSB 862

Prayer

Gracious heavenly Father, we long to see Your Son face-to-face as a bride longs to see her groom. Send Your Son to gather His Church from the ends of the earth to be united with Him in Your eternal kingdom, our heavenly home; through Jesus Christ, Your Son, our Lord, who lives and reigns with You and the Holy Spirit, one God, now and forever. Amen.

Digging Deep
My Personal Study for Week 9

Day 1 • Read 2 Chronicles 29–30

1. How did Hezekiah almost immediately show His dedication to the Lord?

2. The work of the Levites is described as "consecration." What acts of the Levites here help us understand what it means to be consecrated?

3. What types of offerings were the first offered in the newly consecrated temple?

4. Hezekiah's plan to celebrate Passover illustrates a missionary spirit. How did Hezekiah turn the temple and its services into a mission beyond the borders of his kingdom?

5. Reflect on Hezekiah's prayer in 30:18b–19. How does it illustrate the relationship between ritual and heartfelt devotion?

Day 2 • Read 2 Chronicles 31–32

6. How was the success of the consecration and Passover illustrated in the lives of the people?

7. How did the priests and Levites respond?

8. Despite Hezekiah's successes and his faithfulness, his reign was also challenged (ch. 32). Write below the challenger, the setting for the challenge, and the challenger's most striking statement.

Challenger

Setting

Striking Statement

9. How did Hezekiah rise, by faith, to the challenge he faced?

10. *For personal reflection. Sharing optional.* Choose a challenge you face. Drawing on Hezekiah's example, how will you face your challenge?

Day 3 • Read 2 Chronicles 33

11. The next king of Judah enjoyed the longest reign of all Judah's kings. Why might his long reign seem out of place in comparison with the other kings?

12. How do the promises to David and Solomon illustrate the irony of Manasseh's reign?

13. In 2 Chronicles 33:10–16, we begin to understand the reason the Lord allowed Manasseh such a long reign. What events in his life contributed to these circumstances?

14. How was the outcome of Manasseh's life such a contrast to the life of his son and successor, Amon?

15. *For personal reflection. Sharing optional.* We do not know how many years Manasseh spent in depravity. Certainly, his story demonstrates the Lord's patience. Choose someone you know who needs a dramatic change in heart, like Manasseh. Write below an intercessory prayer for that person.

Day 4 • Read 2 Chronicles 34–35

16. After Josiah turned sixteen, what did he do to restore Judah?

17. How did the discovery Hilkiah made ten years later illustrate the extent of the need in Judah?

18. What warning did Huldah the prophetess issue?

19. What promise did Huldah issue?

20. Why did Josiah's righteous reign come to an end?

Physical cause

Spiritual cause

Day 5 • Read 2 Chronicles 36

21. Who were the last four rulers of Judah mentioned by the Chronicler?

22. Judah always stood between two great rival powers in the ancient Near East. Both of these powers are mentioned in chapter 36. List them below.

23. Despite the presence of these mighty kingdoms, they were not the ultimate reason for Judah's downfall. How does the Chronicler explain the fall of the house of David?

24. What happened to the treasures of the house of the Lord?

25. How did the Lord account for the restoration of Judah and the house of David?

12. According to "a man of God," what fear influenced the decisions of Amaziah?

13. How were Amaziah's decisions regarding the gods of Seir especially foolish?

14. How would you interpret the parable told by the king of Israel (25:18)?

15. What did Joash, king of Israel, take from Judah in exchange for the life of King Amaziah?

Day 4 • Read 2 Chronicles 26–27

16. How did Uzziah distinguish himself from his half-hearted father, Amaziah (26:1–15)?

17. What accomplishments are attributed to Uzziah?

18. Why did Jotham need to share the throne with his father, Uzziah, as coregent?

19. What accomplishment did Jotham achieve?

Day 5 • Read 2 Chronicles 28

20. Why was King Ahaz compared with his "father" David rather than with his literal father, King Jotham?

21. What shocking wickedness characterized King Ahaz?

22. The Syro-Ephraimite war was the occasion of one of the Old Testament's most remarkable prophecies. Read Isaiah 7:10–17. What sign would the Lord show to Ahaz?

23. How was this sign to Ahaz ultimately fulfilled? (cf. Matthew 1:22–23).

24. How did the men of Ephraim demonstrate that some leaders in Israel would still honor the Lord with penitent hearts?

11. How were God's justice and mercy manifested in the battle with the Syrians?

Justice

Mercy

12. Compare 2 Chronicles 19:2 with 20:1–4. How did God fulfill the prophetic admonition of Jehu the son of Hanani the seer?

13. How was Jehoshaphat's mission in 2 Chronicles 19:4–7 different from his mission in 17:7–9?

14. What admonitions did Jehoshaphat deliver to the Levites?

Day 4 • Read 2 Chronicles 20

15. What steps did Jehoshaphat take in dealing with challenges the nation faced from the Moabites, Ammonites, and Meunites?

16. When Jehoshaphat prayed for mercy, what reasons did he present to the Lord?

17. How did the people assembled for the fast and prayer illustrate the urgency they felt?

18. Summarize Judah's battle plan.

19. How does the outcome of this battle encourage you to form plans in confronting the difficulties you face?

Day 5 • Read 2 Chronicles 21–22

20. In what remarkable way did Jehoram begin his reign?

21. What "lamp" did the Lord promise to the house of David?

22. How was God's judgment upon Jehoram a fitting response to the way Jehoram began his reign?

23. In 2 Chronicles 18:1, we read about Jehoshaphat's alliance with Ahab. How is the enduring bad fruit of that alliance evident in chapter 22?

24. What heroic deeds rescued the house of David from extinction?

13. Abijah described some unusual ordination practices in the kingdom of Israel. How did these practices illustrate the spiritual problems in Jeroboam's kingdom?

14. What appropriate place does prayer have in battle, then and also today?

Then

Today

15. *For personal reflection. Sharing optional.* How does the example of Abijah inspire and direct you to confront the challenges you face as a believer?

Day 4 • Read 2 Chronicles 14:1–15:7

16. What religious actions formed the heart of Asa's early reign?

17. Considering the example of Asa in 14:6–8, what actions might you take in preparing for the future?

18. How does Asa's prayer in 14:11 describe God?

19. What promises does the Spirit of God deliver through Azariah the son of Obed (15:1–7)?

20. *For personal reflection. Sharing optional.* In view of each promise, what actions might you take in order to reform your own life?

Day 5 • Read 2 Chronicles 15:8–16:14

21. At this point in history, what tribes or portions of tribes dwelled in or came over to the kingdom of Judah?

22. What methods of reform did the people practice or impose during Asa's reform (15:10–15)?

23. What tensions existed between Asa and his mother, the queen?

24. What mistakes did Asa make during the last years of his reign?

25. "There's no fool like an old fool," states an English proverb. Would the mistakes Asa made disqualify him as a good king of Judah? Explain your answer.

Day 3 • Read 2 Chronicles 7

11. How did the Lord show His approval of the temple?

12. a. Who consecrated the temple (7:7)?

b. How was this done?

13. *For personal reflection. Sharing optional.* How does the promise of 7:14 speak to your life?

14. a. According to 7:16, who has consecrated the temple?

b. How does this agree with the answer to question 12?

15. How does 7:19–22 anticipate the experience of the Chronicler's readers?

Day 4 • Read 2 Chronicles 8

16. a. What was the great work Solomon gave himself to, according to 8:3–10?

b. How did Solomon accomplish this work?

17. How does 8:7–8 illustrate a failure on Israel's part?

18. Compare 6:5 with 8:11. How do these passages illustrate how far Israel had come as a nation?

19. Solomon was not the only one with accomplishments. According to 8:14–15, how did others share in the accomplishments?

Day 5 • Read 2 Chronicles 9

20. Why did the Queen of Sheba come to visit Solomon?

21. What did the queen celebrate?

22. a. What does 9:8 tell us about Solomon's influence upon the queen?

b. What lesson could you draw from this for your life?

23. From 9:13–28, choose an accomplishment of Solomon that is most impressive to you. Explain your choice.

24. *For personal reflection. Sharing optional.* Write an accomplishment from your life below, and briefly consider how it brought glory to God, your Maker.

Accomplishment

Glory to God

12. What central message from the Lord and from Solomon is taught in 1:10–12?

13. According to Solomon, what was the purpose of the temple?

14. How do the Lord's message and the purpose of the temple (answers 12 and 13 above) influence your life as a churchgoer?

Day 4 • Read 2 Chronicles 3

15. Compare Genesis 22:2 and 2 Chronicles 3:1. What was significant about the site of the temple?

16. How do Genesis 22:8 and John 1:29 further deepen the importance of this location for our faith?

17. Based on Exodus 25:17–22 and Ezekiel 10:18–19, why were cherubim so important for the decoration of the Most Holy Place in the temple?

Day 5 • Read 2 Chronicles 4

18. a. Based on Exodus 27:1–8 and Leviticus 1, for what purpose was the bronze altar designed?

b. The design changed since Moses' day. Why was a different design necessary?

19. a. What supported the "sea of cast metal" in the temple court (4:2–4)?

b. Read Exodus 20:4–6. How does Solomon's design of the "sea" agree with God's command?

20. The washing of the priests (4:6) anticipates our washing as God's priests in Holy Baptism, as the apostle Peter wrote: "You are a chosen race, a royal priesthood, a holy nation, a people for His own possession, that you may proclaim the excellencies of Him who called you out of darkness into His marvelous light. Once you were not a people, but now you are God's people; once you had not received mercy, but now you have received mercy" (1 Peter 2:9–10). How does the continual need of the priests for washing illustrate our ongoing use for Baptism as Christians?

12. David described new services for the Levites in verses 28–32. List four different examples of such service below.

13. What relationship did the Levites have to the priests, according to verse 32?

Day 4 • Read 1 Chronicles 24–25

14. Read Leviticus 10:1–3 and 1 Chronicles 24:2. Why were Eleazar and Ithamar consecrated as priests?

15. What decision-making tool was used to organize the priests, according to verses 5 and 7?

16. a. The role of singers during the divine service is uniquely described in 1 Chronicles 25:1–2. How are the singers described?

b. What implications does this description have for church services today?

St. Paul writes, "Let the word of Christ dwell in you richly, teaching and admonishing one another in all wisdom, singing psalms and hymns and spiritual songs, with thankfulness in your hearts to God. And whatever you do, in word or deed, do everything in the name of the Lord Jesus, giving thanks to God the Father through Him" (Colossians 3:16–17).

17. What special blessing was promised to Heman, "the king's seer"?

Day 5 • Read 1 Chronicles 26–27

18. What were the duties of a gatekeeper?

19. Read Psalm 84:10. What might this passage tell us about the office of gatekeepers compared with other offices?

20. Read 1 Chronicles 26:20–28. Apart from the house of the Lord being a place of worship, how else was it used?

21. Service at the temple would be based on family divisions. According to 26:29–32, how were other offices filled in David's kingdom?

22. **Challenge question.** Reflect on these different methods for service. What advantages and disadvantages do you see for each one?

b. What lesson should Israel draw from the history?

c. What lesson should the Church draw from this?

14. What two places of worship were approved in Israel before Solomon built the temple?

Day 4 • Read 1 Chronicles 17

15. What issue troubled David?

16. Nathan the prophet spoke for the Lord. What titles did the Lord give to David in 17:7?

17. Based on these titles and verses 8–9, describe David's reign.

18. In a key passage for the entire book, the Lord told David that He "will build you a house" (v. 10). What is meant by "house" in this passage?

19. a. What would the Lord establish forever?

b. How would the Lord fulfill this promise?

20. In David's prayer, he asks three questions (vv. 16, 18, 21). Choose one of these questions, and write an answer to it.

Question

Answer

Day 5 • Read 1 Chronicles 18–20

21. According to chapter 18, what nations did David defeat?

22. What was the cause of David's victories?

23. What insult did the Ammonites show to David's ambassadors?

24. What wisdom did Joab display in his battle with the Ammonites and the Syrians?

25. a. Compare 1 Chronicles 20:1 with 2 Samuel 11:1 and the contents of 2 Samuel 11. What event did the Chronicler omit?

b. Why might the Chronicler have left this event out of his history for the exiles?

10. Zadok the high priest is mentioned in 1 Chronicles 6:53. His descendants served as high priests for about 820 years, from the time of David to the Time between the Testaments. According to 2 Samuel 15:24–37, how did the house of Zadok become such a lasting feature of Israel's leadership?

11. a. Unlike the other tribes of Israel, the Levites did not receive a tribal territory. According to 1 Chronicles 6:54–81, what did the Levites receive?

b. What would be the result of this inheritance?

Day 4 • Read 1 Chronicles 9:35–10:14; 17:1–15

12. The hometown of the first king of Israel and his family is mentioned in 1 Chronicles 9:35. How is this town ideally located for providing a leader to Israel? (You may need to consult a map.)

13. What tragic events are rehearsed in 10:1–7?

14. According to 10:13–14, what two sins led to this tragic result?

15. Israel's next king had plans, but God overturned them (1 Chronicles 17). Why did God do this?

16. The Lord's promises of 17:11–14 are central to the message of Chronicles. How are these promises fulfilled? (Cf. 29:26–28; Matthew 1:18–25.)

Day 5 • Read 1 Chronicles 11–12

17. a. What did the leaders of Israel tell David about this choice of him as king?

b. According to the elders, what did the Lord tell David?

18. Reflect on God's Word to David from 11:2. What does it say about the character of David's reign before God?

19. How did Jerusalem receive the name "city of David"?

20. In 11:10–12:22, the Chronicler describes at least eight different feats of David's mighty men. Summarize below which is your favorite and why it is your favorite.

21. According to 12:23, 38–40, why did troops gather at Hebron?

22. a. David commanded a unique body of men. How does 12:18 illustrate this truth?

b. Can modern troops be similarly clothed and committed? Why or why not?

ASA Seeks the Lord

Asa was the great-grandson of Solomon; he reigned from 911 to 870 BC. Twenty years earlier, his grandfather Rehoboam, at the beginning of his reign, heavily taxed the nation, resulting in a schism (see 2 Chronicles 10). The Southern Kingdom, Judah, remained under the dynasty of David, but the Northern Kingdom, Israel, began a series of nine short dynasties, most of which ended in assassination. The worship of the Northern Kingdom was centered in Dan and Bethel, and it focused on golden calves. Not one king in the north supported the worship of the Lord.

In the south, though, conditions were a bit better. After all, the Judahites retained the capital city of Jerusalem as well as Solomon's temple. Unfortunately, only about half of the kings of Judah were faithful in worshiping the Lord. Asa was one of these.

A Faithful King

At the beginning of Asa's reign, he oversaw many reforms by removing idolatry and unfaithful worship centers. As a result, God gave Asa's people rest from their enemies, and the nation prospered.

But soon there was a crisis. An army of one million Cushites (or Ethiopians) with chariots marched against Asa's army of 580,000. The chances of victory were slim to none, but Asa sought the Lord for deliverance. He prayed, "O Lord, there is none like You to help, between the mighty and the weak. Help us, O Lord our God, for we rely on You" (2 Chronicles 14:11). And with the blessing of God, the enemy was defeated, and Israel received much plunder.

After Asa's success, a Word from the Lord came through the prophet Azariah: "The Lord is with you while you are with Him. If you seek Him, He will be found by you, but if you forsake Him, He will forsake you" (2 Chronicles 15:2). The admonition to "seek the Lord" is a key to understanding Asa's life; in fact, the word "seek" is found nine times in the texts about Asa. This crucial phrase repeats one of the four key ideas in 2 Chronicles 7:14: "If My people who are called by My name humble themselves, and pray and *seek* My face and turn from their wicked ways, then I will hear from heaven and will forgive their sin and heal their land."

Seek First

To seek God means to put Him first in our lives. Jesus tell us, "But seek first the kingdom of God and His righteousness" (Matthew 6:33). Let's spell out **F-I-R-S-T** to see how we can follow in Asa's footsteps.

Finances: The Bible says, "Honor the Lord with your wealth and with the firstfruits of all your produce" (Proverbs 3:9). We Americans are consumed with consuming. To give some perspective, in 1980, 30 percent of all income was spent on luxuries, or about 350 billion dollars. Now that figure is up to 38 percent, or about 500 billion dollars annually spent on "fun." What about us? How do we spend our money?

Interests: St. Paul writes, "So, whether you eat or drink, or whatever you do, do all to the glory of God" (1 Corinthians 10:31). Are my hobbies and recreational activities God-pleasing? What sorts of books and magazines do I like?

Relationships: Scripture says, "Do not be deceived: 'Bad company ruins good morals'" (1 Corinthians 15:33). We become like the people we spend the most time with. Who are my friends? What are their priorities in life? Do I need to make some tough decisions in this area?

Schedule: The apostle admonishes us to go through our days "making the best use of the time, because the days are evil" (Ephesians 5:16). What does my use of time say about my priorities? What does my daily planner say about me?

Trouble: God invites us to "call upon Me in the day of trouble; I will deliver you, and you shall glorify Me" (Psalm 50:15). Whom do I go to when I am devastated or depressed? Do I turn to the pseudo-saviors and false hopes offered by the world?

Right after Asa began to seek the Lord, the king made some drastic decisions. He removed the idols from his land and repaired the Lord's altar. He then gathered people to worship the Lord, not just from Judah but also many from the Northern Kingdom. Years of rivalry were overcome because the people were seeking God. Thousands of sacrifices were offered, and people made a covenant "to seek the Lord, the God of their fathers, with all their heart and with all their soul" (2 Chronicles 15:12). Seeking the Lord with all his heart, Asa even deposed Maacah, the queen mother (Asa's grandmother), who had made a pagan idol, "a detestable image for Asherah" (v. 16).

An Unfaithful King

Unfortunately, during the next twenty-five years of peace, Asa slowly fell away from the Lord and began to seek other things besides his God. So when he faced another crisis, with Israel threatening him from the north, instead of going to the Lord for help, he paid the pagan nation of Aram to be his ally and help him fight. Once again, a prophet reminded Asa of God's help in the past and warned him of God's judgment. But the king's reaction this time was much different. He imprisoned the prophet and brutally oppressed his own people.

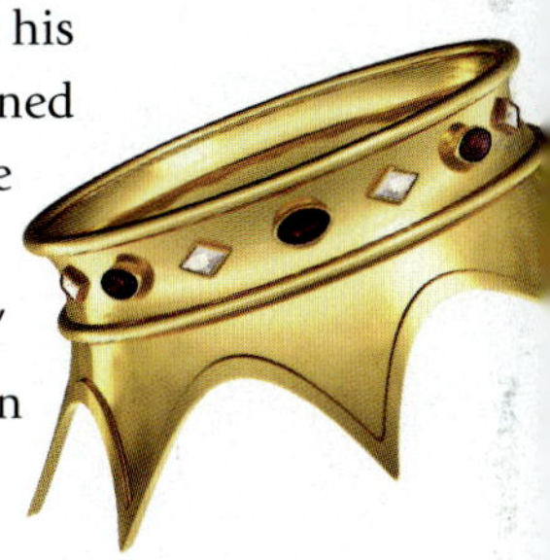

Later, when struck with sickness, he "did not seek the Lord, but sought help from physicians" (2 Chronicles 16:12), who perhaps used magic at that time in an attempt to heal people. To turn to physicians was like turning against God to pagan gods for healing. Two years later, Asa died.

Learning from Asa

This is a sad ending to a king who had been a great man of God. Yet, the same thing that happened to Asa can happen to us. During a crisis, we seek the Lord; but gradually during times of peace, we often turn back to our old ways. It's usually not overnight, but we spend less and less time in God's Word and seeking His will.

What can we learn from King Asa? We can learn to seek Jesus with *all* our heart for *all* of our days. After all, only Jesus is our doorway to deliverance, our pathway to peace, and our gateway to glory. His mercy is matchless. His goodness is limitless. His love never changes. His grace is sufficient. His Word is enough. And His reign is righteous forevermore! All of these gifts are ours, *today*. Let's trust Him when He says, "But seek first the kingdom of God and His righteousness, and all these things will be added to you" (Matthew 6:33).

JEHOSHAPHAT Prays to the Lord

Jehoshaphat reigned from 873 to 848 BC and was one of Judah's most faithful kings. It was therefore a terrible shock when the report came that a great army from three nations had gathered on the border of Judah to invade God's people. Never before in his reign of nearly twenty peaceful years had King Jehoshaphat faced such a crisis. Certainly the end of Judah appeared imminent.

When Jehoshaphat received this terrible news, he was "afraid and set his face to seek the Lord, and proclaimed a fast throughout all Judah" (2 Chronicles 20:3). Jehoshaphat had never faced such a challenge. What could have brought on this sudden change of events? Could it have been his recent association with the wicked Northern King Ahab (2 Chronicles 18)?

Not knowing why his life was crumbling before his very eyes, Jehoshaphat's reaction was to pray.

Calling upon the Lord

This was precisely what God had asked of His people in 2 Chronicles 7:14: "If My people who are called by My name humble themselves, and *pray* and seek My face and turn from their wicked ways, then I will hear from heaven and will forgive their sin and heal their land." In Jehoshaphat's prayer, he uttered these words to the Lord: "O Lord, God of our fathers, are You not God in heaven? You rule over all the kingdoms of the nations. In Your hand are power and might, so that none is able to withstand You" (2 Chronicles 20:6). The king confesses that God's hands are mighty to save.

© iStockphoto.com

After all, these are the hands that made the world and direct history. The Lord's hand is never too weak to save.

Several additional characteristics of Jehoshaphat's prayer need to be emphasized. First, it was not limited to a certain group or even age. He invited all people and all ages to participate, even if they were unable to understand what was being said (e.g., infants). It was not unusual for children to participate in national meetings in the Old Testament.

Second, the king's prayer focused almost entirely on glorifying God and lifting up His Word. A list of requests was not the focus; instead, Jehoshaphat simply repeated to God who He was: "God of our fathers," "God in heaven," the one who "rule[s] over all the kingdoms of the nations" (2 Chronicles 20:6). Jehoshaphat reiterated what the Lord had done and reminded Him of His promises.

> *Did You not, our God, drive out the inhabitants of this land before Your people Israel, and give it forever to the descendants of Abraham Your friend? And they have lived in it and have built for You in it a sanctuary for Your name, saying, "If disaster comes upon us, the sword, judgment, or pestilence, or famine, we will stand before this house and before You—for Your name is in this house—and cry out to You in our affliction, and You will hear and save."* (2 Chronicles 20:7–9)

Third, Jehoshaphat admitted before God and the entire nation that he didn't have the answers: "For we are powerless against this great horde that is coming against us. We do not know what to do, but our eyes are on You" (2 Chronicles 20:12).

The king and all the people were before the Lord in prayer when this message was given by a prophet: "'You will not need to fight in this battle. Stand firm, hold your position, and see the salvation of the LORD on your behalf, O Judah and Jerusalem.' Do not be afraid and do not be dismayed. Tomorrow go out against them, and the LORD will be with you" (2 Chronicles 20:17). The battle belongs to the Lord!

This promise set off a chain of events that are absolutely amazing. The words of God touched their hearts so deeply that the entire nation began to praise Him to an extent that was rarely seen in the Old Testament. First, the king and all inhabitants of Jerusalem fell down to the ground in spontaneous worship. Then at the same time, two families of the Levites stood up. They were the ones in charge of the holiest parts of the temple (Kohathites) and those famous for their many songs of praise (Korahites). They worshiped the Lord with a "very loud voice" (2 Chronicles 20:19).

Marching into Battle

The next morning, as the nation was to march into battle, the king again repeated God's promise and then ordered the army to march in a procession unheard of before, with singers going first! As they marched down from Jerusalem to Engedi, where the enemy multitudes were waiting, the choir was the first in line, singing, "Give thanks to the LORD, for His steadfast love endures forever" (2 Chronicles 20:21).

Scripture describes God at work through these Israelites who praised the Lord: "And when they began to sing and praise, the LORD set an ambush against the men of Ammon, Moab, and Mount Seir, who had come against Judah" (2 Chronicles 20:22). The enemy army began destroying itself, and by the time Judah was able to see their enemy, "there were dead bodies lying on the ground; none had escaped" (2 Chronicles 20:24).

What had the Israelites done? They had simply prayed and praised God—and nothing more. The people placed everything in His hands.

Safe in the Hands of God

What is our response when the enemies of faith, hope, and love crash into our lives? We, too, are invited to place ourselves into God's hands.

Jesus often demonstrated His power and authority by doing miracles with His hands. For instance, to a leper who asked if He was willing to heal Him, "Jesus stretched out His hand and touched him, saying, 'I will; be clean'" (Matthew 8:3). On another occasion, the Savior said, "I give them eternal life, and they will never perish, and no one will snatch them out of My hand" (John 10:28). But Christ's most deliberate show of hands was on Good Friday, when He stretched them out on a Roman cross. Spit, sweat, and blood were caked to those hands. They were pierced with iron nails. They bled as death twanged her morbid melody. Yet, three days later, coming forth alive from the tomb, Jesus showed these same loving hands to His disciples. In prayer, just like Jehoshaphat, we may place ourselves into God's hands, which keep us safe in His love forever!

THE ASSYRIAN EMPIRE

The Book of 2 Chronicles details for us the history of the Southern Kingdom of Judah, from the time of Solomon until the end of the Babylonian captivity. One of the nations that takes center stage in the Book of 2 Chronicles is Assyria. Assyria was a mighty empire that dominated the Middle East from the ninth through seventh centuries BC. The heartland of this nation included the ancient cites of Ashur, Erbil, Nineveh, and Calah. Over time, the Assyrians were able to conquer a large empire, stretching from Egypt in the west to Persia in the east and from the Persian Gulf in the south to Asia Minor in the north. This terrifying pagan nation was raised up by God to be His instrument of judgment—and also to serve as a demonstration of His mercy.

Iñigo Quintanilla/Hemera/Thinkstock

An Unstoppable War Machine

The Assyrians were known principally for fielding a truly formidable army that swept away all of its opposition. There were a couple of reasons for this. Most scholars today believe that the Assyrians fielded the world's first truly integrated operational army. Their army had various specialized units that acted in mutually supporting roles. There have been many bas-reliefs excavated from ancient Assyrian palaces, many of which have images that depict their army of this time. There are scenes of archers firing their arrows from behind the shields of spearmen. Depictions of Assyrian cavalry show pairs of horses harnessed together, with a rider on each. One rider would guide the team with reigns while the other rider was an archer who would shoot arrows from horseback.

The Assyrians were also experts at siege warfare. Ancient cities were protected by walls and towers. It took a determined enemy with considerable technical skill to breach the walls and fight its way into such cities. The Assyrians employed various siege engines as well as ladders and battering rams. They also had troops trained as sappers and miners who would attempt to either tunnel under the walls or bore their way through the mud-brick walls with poles. In its heyday, the Assyrian army had no peers.

Systematic Cruelty

The Assyrians were also known for their unyielding cruelty to their captives. In fact, they were quite proud of their cruelty and made monuments celebrating that fact. Prisoners and captive people were routinely deported from their ancestral lands to distant provinces of the empire. Often, they would be marched away, a long line of captives chained together by the nose. In some cases, the bones of their ancestors would first be dug up and destroyed in their presence. These practices demonstrated to the captives that they no longer had a home or a history; they were no longer a nation or a people. They were merely part of the servile population of the Assyrian Empire.

There was, of course, a method to Assyria's madness. Such cruelty made it far less likely that any of the conquered peoples would rebel against them. Also, it made for easier conquests. The Assyrians' cruelty to the people of defeated cities was so well known that cities would often simply surrender when they heard of the approach of the imperial army. It was better to negotiate terms of surrender than to hold out for a brief time and then be completely destroyed. The Assyrians were a terrifying foe.

Psychological Warfare

An example of an Assyrian tactic that could be described as psychological warfare took place in 701 BC, when Assyria invaded the Southern Kingdom of Judah during the reign of King Hezekiah. Although these events are related to us in 2 Chronicles 32, we find even more detail in 2 Kings 18–19.

The Rabshakeh, an Assyrian officer, was sent to Jerusalem to speak to the defenders and demand their surrender:

And the Rabshakeh said to them, "Say to Hezekiah, 'Thus says the great king, the king of Assyria: On what do you rest this trust of yours? Do you think that mere words are strategy and power for war? In whom do you now trust, that you have rebelled against me? Behold, you are trusting now in Egypt, that broken reed of a staff, which will pierce the hand of any man who leans on it. Such is Pharaoh king of Egypt to all who trust in him. But if you say to me, "We trust in the LORD our God," is it not He whose high places and altars Hezekiah has removed, saying to Judah and to Jerusalem, "You shall worship before this altar in Jerusalem"? Come now, make a wager with my master the king of Assyria: I will give you two thousand horses, if you are able on your part to set riders on them. How then can you repulse a single captain among the least of my master's servants, when you trust in Egypt for chariots and for horsemen? Moreover, is it without the LORD that I have come up against this place to destroy it? The LORD said to me, Go up against this land, and destroy it.'"

Then Eliakim the son of Hilkiah, and Shebnah, and Joah, said to the Rabshakeh, "Please speak to your servants in Aramaic, for we understand it. Do not speak to us in the language of Judah within the hearing of the people who are on the wall." But the Rabshakeh said to them, "Has my master sent me to speak these words to your master and to you, and not to the men sitting on the wall, who are doomed with you to eat their own dung and to drink their own urine?"

Then the Rabshakeh stood and called out in a loud voice in the language of Judah: "Hear the word of the great king, the king of Assyria! Thus says the king: 'Do not let Hezekiah deceive you, for he will not be able to deliver you out of my hand.'" (2 Kings 18:19–29)

This passage gives us some amazing details of Assyrian tactics and intelligence gathering. Assyria was well aware of Judah's attempts to enlist Egypt as an ally. Assyria also knew of Hezekiah's efforts to destroy the pagan shrines at the high places and other locations throughout Judah. The Assyrian officer (Rabshakeh) also insisted on speaking his message in Hebrew (the common language understood by all the defenders) rather than Aramaic (a language understood by the more educated officers and members of the king's court). The Assyrian officer was not just trying to convince King Hezekiah to surrender; he was also trying to demoralize as many of the common soldiers as possible.

God's Judgment and Mercy

These are the people who God raised up to be His instrument of judgment. As a punishment for the people's idolatry and their persistent refusal to repent, the Lord caused the Assyrian Empire to conquer and assimilate the Northern Kingdom. The people were led off into captivity, deported to other provinces within the empire, and never returned to the Promised Land.

In reading of the Assyrian invasion of the Southern Kingdom of Judah, we see that the unstoppable Assyrians were, in fact, stopped and even pushed back. At the height of the crisis, the Lord heard the prayers of King Hezekiah and Isaiah the Prophet:

> *And the Lord sent an angel, who cut off all the mighty warriors and commanders and officers in the camp of the king of Assyria. So he returned with shame of face to his own land. And when he came into the house of his god, some of his own sons struck him down there with the sword. So the Lord saved Hezekiah and the inhabitants of Jerusalem from the hand of Sennacherib king of Assyria and from the hand of all his enemies, and He provided for them on every side.* (2 Chronicles 32:21–22)

The almighty power of God was seen in His mercy to His people when He stopped the unstoppable enemy.

Robert Papp/© CPH

HEZEKIAH Turns to the Lord

The reign of King Hezekiah (715–686 BC) can best be characterized by the phrase "turn from their wicked ways." He grew up during very unstable times, both politically and spiritually. The Assyrian Empire to the north was on the brink of invading the Northern Kingdom of Israel. By 732 BC, Assyria had conquered that country's northern tribes, and in only ten more years, it would invade and destroy the entire Northern Kingdom. The people of Judah had to wonder if they would be Assyria's next victims.

What was more difficult to endure, though, for Hezekiah, was the apostate leadership of his father, King Ahaz. During Ahaz's reign (735–715 BC), he made idols to Baal and Molech, burned incense "under every green tree," and even burned some of his sons as sacrifices to the pagan gods. Thus, the Lord allowed Judah to suffer under the attack of all the nations surrounding them. Did this humiliation cause Ahaz to return to God? No. He worshiped the gods of the nations that attacked him, made sacrifices to idols, closed the temple, and built pagan altars in every place in Jerusalem.

From the first day of Hezekiah's reign, however, he began to turn his nation from idolatry back to the Lord. He, like faithful kings before him, embraced the promises in 2 Chronicles 7:14: "If My people who are called by My name humble themselves, and pray and seek My face and *turn from their wicked ways*, then I will hear from heaven and will forgive their sin and heal their land."

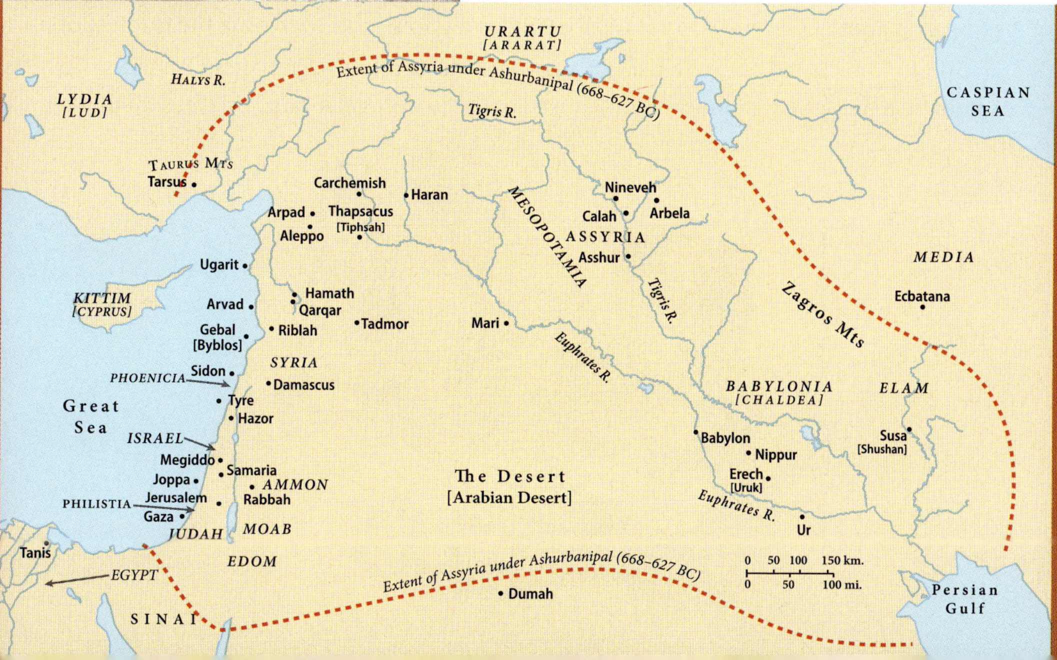

Godly ABCs

Hezekiah turned from the evil ways of his father, Ahaz. The Bible says, "In the first year of his reign, in the first month, he opened the doors of the house of the LORD and repaired them" (2 Chronicles 29:3). Then, Hezekiah gave a speech to the Levites, explaining the reason why there had been so much disaster and crisis in the country: their nation had turned away from God. He challenged these leaders to return to their calling of serving the Lord. If we could summarize what it looks like to turn from sinful ways, what would that look like? Consider these "ABCs" of turning to God.

A: Admit our problem. Scripture says, "Whoever conceals his transgressions will not prosper, but he who confesses and forsakes them will obtain mercy" (Proverbs 28:13). We need to stop living in denial and face the truth of our bad decisions and lackluster faith.

B: Believe in change. James and John were once called the Sons of Thunder. Jesus softens hard hearts—James and John went on to become loving and compassionate Christians.

C: Claim forgiveness. "If we confess our sins, He is faithful and just to forgive us our sins and to cleanse us from all unrighteousness" (1 John 1:9). Through our faith in the Savior, God indeed forgives us all of our sins.

Turning to God is as uncomplicated as ABC!

Renewal of God's People

Just ask Hezekiah's Levitical leaders! Turning to the Lord through their king's leadership, the Levites assembled all their brothers and went to work for sixteen days, cleansing, repairing, and consecrating the once-desecrated temple.

But this was only the beginning of the turning. Hezekiah's vision reached far beyond Jerusalem to the entire kingdom, including the north. The king wanted to bring renewal to all the people of God by sending out an invitation for the people of the Northern Kingdom to turn from unbelief back to the Lord and to come to Jerusalem to celebrate the Passover. It was a bold plan that had not been realized since the days of Solomon, over 250 years earlier.

What was the response of those in the Northern Kingdom? Most rejected and laughed at this message. But some from Manasseh, Asher, and Zebulon turned from their evil ways and worshiped the Lord. This was not an easy step after 200 years of bitter rivalry, but God's Spirit can overcome the greatest of obstacles.

In preparation for this sacred event, Jerusalem was cleansed of all its pagan altars. Then the first Passover lambs to be known in many generations were sacrificed as the people celebrated this festival that represented

Marina Mariya/iStock/Thinkstock

the redemption and birth of the nation. Many who had long forgotten the Lord turned to serve Him.

A striking characteristic of this Passover was that traditional rules were broken. First, the Passover was held one month later than the proper date. It was like celebrating Christmas Eve on January 24. It just didn't make sense to wait another year for this celebration when the people were ready to turn to God at that moment.

Second, many worshipers came without being "sanctified." Apparently, it had been so long since many of these Israelites had brought sacrifices that they forgot the law concerning spiritual purity (ceremonial washing, avoiding unclean things). Therefore, the king interceded for them before God as the crowds spontaneously came to worship the Lord.

The celebration of the festival of Unleavened Bread was also an occasion to bend the rules. Normally, this was held for just one week following Passover; but because it was such a joyful celebration, "the whole assembly agreed together to keep the feast for another seven days. So they kept it for another seven days with gladness" (2 Chronicles 30:23). After these meetings of unbridled gladness, God's people left Jerusalem and systematically cleansed the nation from any idols, altars, or remnants of pagan worship. The turn from wicked ways was complete!

Finally, at the request of Hezekiah, contributions were taken to provide for the ministry of the temple. "As soon as the command was spread abroad, the people of Israel gave in abundance the firstfruits of grain, wine, oil, honey, and of all the produce of the field. And they brought in abundantly the tithe of everything" (2 Chronicles 31:5). So great was the response that the overabundance of offerings had to be piled in heaps for four months!

Renewed through the Eternal Passover Lamb

A year earlier, the people had been walking in dread of the Assyrians and were spiritually dead. The people from the Northern Kingdom had been worshiping pagan idols. What changed these people?

Through the leadership of King Hezekiah, the people turned from their wicked ways and returned to the Lord. Hezekiah admitted the wickedness of his father, Ahaz, believed the Lord could change the nation, and claimed God's forgiving love, sealed in the Passover lamb. Through these same ABCs, we also can gladly turn to our God and enjoy the blessings of the eternal Passover, "for Christ, our Passover lamb, has been sacrificed" (1 Corinthians 5:7).

JOSIAH Is Humble before the Lord

Josiah was only eight years old when he began his reign as one of the last but greatest kings of Judah. Ruling from 640 to 609 BC, Josiah "did what was right in the eyes of the LORD, and walked in the ways of David his father; and he did not turn aside to the right hand or to the left" (2 Chronicles 34:2). By the age of sixteen, he "began to seek the God of David his father" (2 Chronicles 34:3). Just like Hezekiah, his great-grandfather before him, Josiah grew up in terribly immoral circumstances. Manasseh, his grandfather, was one of Judah's most wicked kings, and Amon, Josiah's father, followed in Manasseh's footsteps.

Both Manasseh and Amon worshiped the Canaanite deities Baal and Asherah. What was it that made these pagan gods so tempting? Judah had no major source of water. Mesopotamian empires like Assyria and Babylon thrived off of the Tigris and Euphrates Rivers, while Egypt's source of life was the Nile River. Judah, on the other hand, was completely dependent upon rain for her source of moisture. This is where Baal and Asherah came in. Ancient texts from Ugarit (in present-day northern Lebanon) picture Baal as the provider of rain. He would send rain when a man went to a "high place," enlisted a "sacred" prostitute (much like Gomer may have been in Hosea 1), and had sex with her. The pagans believed that this would prompt Baal to engage in sex with the goddess Asherah, which would then produce rain.

With Josiah seeing his nation about to be destroyed by this idolatry, he trusted in the words of 2 Chronicles 7:14: "If My people who are called by My name *humble themselves*, and pray and seek My face and turn from their wicked ways, then I will hear from heaven and will forgive their sin and heal their land." While pride says, "There is another way," humility confesses, "I will walk in God's way."

Walking in God's Way

Humble before his God, Josiah was ready to meet the challenges of idolatry head on. When he was twenty-one, the king began to cleanse the nation of Baal and Asherah. "He began to purge Judah and Jerusalem of the high places, the Asherim, and the carved and the metal images" (2 Chronicles 34:3). He ordered people to chop down Baal's altars and cut down the Asherah poles. Josiah was so zealous for the Lord that the pagan priests were killed and their bones were burned on their altars. The king even carried his reformation into regions north of Judah.

Josiah's humility prompted him to make more reforms. He collected money to repair and cleanse the temple. What the king didn't realize was that by doing so, he would discover the long-lost Word of God. According to Deuteronomy 31:26, God's Word was to be placed by the side of the ark of the covenant. Apparently, over time, the priests who were responsible for the scrolls forgot where they were. It seems difficult to picture a time when God's Word was entirely lost. But that is what idolatry does. Amos had prophesied many years earlier that this would happen: "'Behold, the days are coming,' declares the Lord God, 'when I will send a famine on the land—not a famine of bread, nor a thirst for water, but of hearing the words of the Lord'" (Amos 8:11).

Imagine Josiah's surprise when he heard a report about the temple work and, at the very end, Shaphan the secretary told him, "Hilkiah the priest has given me a book" (2 Chronicles 34:18). Two aspects of this event immediately make an impression. First, that the Word of God was so unknown that when it was discovered, it was just considered a book like any other. Second, this "book" was mentioned only after the building and treasury report.

Josiah, on the other hand, knew exactly what had been discovered, and he immediately ordered the messenger to read the Scripture in its entirety. What did he read? It was at least the Book of Deuteronomy, if not all five of the books of Moses: Genesis, Exodus, Leviticus, Numbers, and Deuteronomy. The impression of the Scripture on Josiah was unbelievable: "And when the king

Shlomo Polonsky/Hemera/Thinkstock

heard the words of the Law, he tore his clothes" and "wept" (2 Chronicles 34:19, 27). As the reformers once wrote, "God works through this means (i.e., the preaching and hearing of His Word). He breaks our hearts [Jeremiah 4:3–4] and draws us to Him [John 6:44]. Through the preaching of the Law, a person comes to know his sins and God's wrath. He experiences in his heart true terrors, contrition, and sorrow" (*Concordia: The Lutheran Confessions*, second ed. [St. Louis: Concordia, 2006], Formula of Concord, Solid Declaration, II:54). Josiah was crushed by the law of judgment and therefore cried out to God in repentance.

The king's humble heart points to another King, whose humility not only changed a nation but also changed the whole world. Paul writes of Jesus, "who, though He was in the form of God, did not count equality with God a thing to be grasped, but made Himself nothing, taking the form of a servant, being born in the likeness of men. And being found in human form, He humbled Himself by becoming obedient to the point of death, even death on a cross" (Philippians 2:6–8). Although He is almighty, Jesus cried. Although He is the owner of all things, He said, "Foxes have holes, and birds of the air have nests, but the Son of Man has nowhere to lay His head" (Matthew 8:20). Although He is the King of kings, He became a servant. The Creator, He was spit on by the creatures. The source of truth, He was declared guilty of a lie. The source of light, He hung in the darkness for three hours. The source of life, He was crucified, died, and was buried. Jesus went from the pinnacle of praise in the universe to the ultimate, absolute nothing. "He had no form or majesty that we should look at Him, and no beauty that we should desire Him" (Isaiah 53:2).

Jozef Sedmak/Hemera/Thinkstock

Exalted by the Mighty Hand of God

The temptation to go our own way is always before us. The temptation to forget and even to lose the Word of God is also always present. The pride of our sinful nature continually entices us away from following God's way to follow something that seems better or more satisfying to us. Ultimately, what we are doing is engaging in a form of idolatry, not unlike the people of ancient Judah.

It is a humble soul that turns from its own path to follow one laid out by another. Through Josiah's humility, the land of Judah was cleansed of idols and God's Word was restored. Because of Christ's humility, we are cleansed of our sin and delight in Holy Scripture, even as we embrace this truth. "Humble yourselves, therefore, under the mighty hand of God so that at the proper time He may exalt you" (1 Peter 5:6).

iStock/Thinkstock